Sein Off

The Final Days of *Seinfeld*

How does it feel to say good-bye to nine years of the funniest and most successful television show in history? For *Seinfeld*'s creators and stars, it was painful, joyous, hilarious, and filled with emotion.

Pulitzer Prize–winning photographer David Hume Kennerly teamed up with Jerry, Julia, Michael, and Jason for the poignant final days of the show. The result? *SeinOff*, a visual documentary of one of America's classic comedy teams performing for the very last time.

Kennerly was given unlimited access on the set, capturing the explosive last laughs and precious private moments. His more than 150 stunning, never-before-seen images are both lighthearted and dramatic. The cast's revealing and touching commentary will take you on a personal tour of their final days.

SeinOff is an exploration of what life was like off-camera and behind the scenes. It gives audiences exclusive insight into how the ensemble related to one another, to their characters, and what the show that defined the '90s has meant to them.

Sein Off

The Final Days of *Seinfeld*

by:
Jerry Seinfeld

Julia Louis-Dreyfus

Michael Richards

and Jason Alexander

photographs by:
David Hume Kennerly/*Newsweek*

picture editor:
Jain Lemos

text editor:
Todd Gold

book design:
Erbe Design, South Pasadena, CA

photographic printing:
Paris Photo Lab, Los Angeles, CA

HarperEntertainment
An Imprint of HarperCollinsPublishers
http://www.harpercollins.com

by: Jerry Seinfeld, Julia Louis-Dreyfus,
  Michael Richards, and Jason Alexander

photographs by: David Hume Kennerly/*Newsweek*

picture editor: Jain Lemos

text editor: Todd Gold

book design and production: Maureen Erbe,
  Natalie Erbe, Efi Latief, Rita Sowins: Erbe Design,
  South Pasadena, CA

photographic printing: Paris Photo Lab,
  Los Angeles, CA

HarperCollins books may be purchased for educational,
business, or sales promotional use. For information please
write: Special Markets Department, HarperCollins
Publishers, Inc., 10 East 53rd Street, New York, NY 10022.

FIRST EDITION

ISBN 0-06-055376-6 (hardcover)

ISBN 0-06-095328-4 (paperback)

98 99 00 01 02/WZ 10 9 8 7 6 5 4 3 2 1

Introduction

I photograph history for a living. That's been my profession for over thirty years. I've documented seven United States presidents and hundreds of world leaders. I have witnessed some of the biggest events of my generation—the Vietnam War, Robert Kennedy's assassination, the Amazin' Mets winning the 1969 World Series, Richard Nixon's resignation, the Jonestown massacre, Reagan's and Gorbachev's Fireside Summit, starvation in isolated North Korea, and much more. When I heard that *Seinfeld* was ending, I knew I had to be there!

I then suggested the idea of shooting an in-depth, behind-the-scenes photographic essay of the final days of *Seinfeld* to *Newsweek* magazine, but I met some skepticism. "Sure, go right ahead," they said. "If you can gain access to the hottest entertainment story of the decade, we'll be happy to run it." Everyone was clamoring for pictures of this big television event, but nobody was going to get inside.

I decided to go directly to the source, so I sent Jerry Seinfeld a copy of my book *Photo Op*, a volume of photographs I had taken over a twenty-five-year period. To offset the wars and disasters it contained, I included a funny picture that I had taken of Hillary Clinton wincing. Underneath the photo I jokingly wrote, "No more *Seinfeld*?" I explained to Jerry that I would like to shoot the finale from an historical perspective. I also assured him that I was capable of photographing subjects other than bullets, bodies, and men in gray suits. Jerry liked my approach and invited me along for the last ride. It was quite a trip.

I photographed the final days of *Seinfeld* the same way I would a big political story. The elements were similar—famous personalities doing something extremely difficult under tremendous stress and intense public scrutiny. My challenge has always been to show the human side of people. I tried to capture a sense of what they were thinking and feeling as they won or lost an election, signed a pardon, sent men and women into battle, or, as in this case, gathered for the last time to finish a long-running hit series.

"No more *Seinfeld*?"

America watched *Seinfeld* for nine years. Fans knew all about Jerry, George, Elaine, and Kramer, but what about the real Jerry, Jason, Julia, and Michael? How did they feel about walking out of Jerry's living room set for the last time? Was it hard? Easy? Did they really like one another or was there tension on the set? Pictures, in this case anyway, do help tell the story, particularly when accompanied by the insightful comments by those who lived through it.

The surprises started the first day I arrived on the set. I was expecting the *Seinfeld* actors to be suspicious of me since I had virtually unheard-of access to take pictures anytime, anywhere. I expected them to bolt whenever I approached them. But they didn't. Everyone on the set was friendly and down-to-earth. I found Jerry Seinfeld warm, professional, and one of the most well adjusted people I have ever met. On that very first day, things got off to a great start when I photographed Jerry and his friend Mario Joyner sharing an explosively funny moment, ending with Jerry doubled over with laughter and then wiping tears from his eyes (pages 18–21).

Jason Alexander (George), the only one of the group I'd met before, always had a mischievous gleam in his eye and a quick smile for friends and strangers alike. I had the feeling that

Jason had prankster's blood coursing through his veins (page 53).

Julia Louis-Dreyfus (Elaine) balanced her duties as a mom with one of the most eccentric women's roles on television. She's a cross between a young Elizabeth Taylor and Lucille Ball (pages 22–23). I knew she was a great actress, but I realized she had exquisite taste as well when she exhibited wild enthusiasm for the pictures I was taking and thought they should be made into a book!

Meeting Michael Richards (Kramer) was the biggest surprise of all. He is nothing like his character on the show. Michael is a shy, quiet-spoken man and one of the most talented and hardest-working people I have ever run into. He pours every ounce of his energy into his acting. One of the best shots I took was from behind the door of Jerry's apartment as he rushed at it a split second before bursting through to the other side (pages 56–57). That entrance has become a television classic.

The only hint of suspicion toward me came from *Seinfeld* cocreator Larry David. He had left *Seinfeld* two years earlier, but returned to write and oversee "The Finale." He was understand-ably nervous and had no time for interlopers. Larry didn't want any outsiders inside, and that included me. In a lighthearted attempt to put him at ease when we were introduced just before the highly classified table reading of the final script, I said, "I'm probably the only person in this room who has had a top secret clearance. I didn't talk about Brezhnev, and I sure as hell ain't discussing *Seinfeld*." He laughed. After that I was in the clear.

There was one moment that Jerry didn't want photographed. Before every audience show, the four actors would huddle offstage while Jerry gave them a short pep talk. This ritual ended in a shout, like athletes preparing to go onto the field. I wanted to document that moment, but Jerry said no, it was too private. I said, "Why not let me shoot it and you can decide later whether or not it will ever be published" (pages 152–153).

The astronomical ratings that *Seinfeld* garnered in its final year suggested that many Americans cared more about what Jerry & Co. were doing every week than even the trials and tribulations of the president. The pictures in this book take a serious look at the end of an important chapter of American cultural history. This is the first time that a popular televi-sion production has been documented in this fashion. It's a shame that no similar record exists of *I Love Lucy, The Mary Tyler Moore Show, M.A.S.H., Taxi*, and some of the other great shows of this century.
—David Hume Kennerly

Jeff MacNelly is a three-time Pulitzer Prize–winning editorial cartoonist who also draws Shoe. Here, he puts his friend Kennerly into proper perspective.

Kennerly won a Pulitzer Prize for his Vietnam pictures, was personal photog-rapher to President Gerald R. Ford, and has traveled to more than 140 countries on assignment. He is a contributing editor for Newsweek magazine, where he shoots wars, politics, and the demise of popular sitcoms.

Jerry: One of the main reasons you become a stand-up comic is that you don't work well with others. Yet in television you need a lot of people to get the job done each week. I'd say it's the most collaborative medium in entertainment. Here, the show's writers and I are working on "The Puerto Rican Day," the last regular episode of *Seinfeld*. Writing jokes is not a pretty sight. A joke is not a flowing thought, it's like a "clean and jerk" in weightlifting. Either you lift it or you don't. There's no middle ground with a joke—it works or it doesn't, which can be frustrating. That's why when you hit the right note, laughter is such a joyous release.

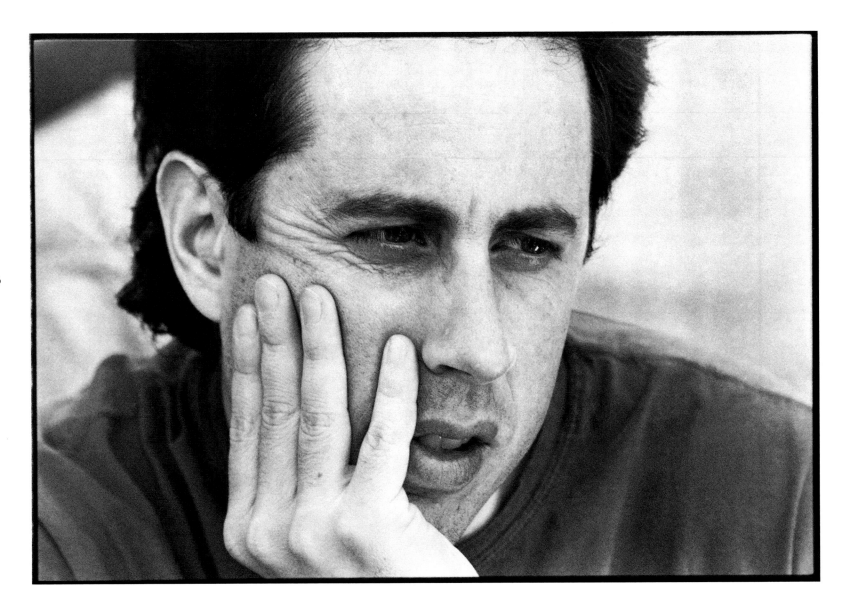

Jerry: *Seinfeld* is something I learned to do because I was given the opportunity. Then the show spiraled off into this whole other entity that I knew I had to serve because it had its own desire to be something. The experience was just the most amazing rocket ride.

Julia: During the last week of shooting, I was struck by the fact that Elaine was one of the best female characters ever written for television, and I'm grateful to have been lucky enough to play her. Gender was never a deterrent to the comedy of Elaine. All of the characters found great strength in their weaknesses, Elaine included. There were no biases of any sort. She was as big a buffoon as the rest of them.

Jason: George got unhealthier over the years. Even in his deepest core of angst and anger, I admired his ability to step back and see the humor of it all. That was his healthiest and most endearing attribute. He did things I'd never do. He yelled at people on the street. I lived vicariously through George, even though he didn't fare well. I think that was part of his appeal. When people reflected on their own lives in comparison to George's, they felt pretty good. No matter how bad life may have been for any given member of our audience, they could tune in and see it was far worse for this poor slob. In a sick way that was comforting.

Michael: Kramer came naturally to me. But I really had to stay on top of this guy. Right up until the finale, I'd constantly ask myself, "Is he too big, too broad?" I never wanted to turn him into a cartoon. But I liked how Kramer would go into different characters. I liked how he schemed. I enjoyed when he'd do something to get the others out of trouble. He delighted in everything. He was truly absorbed in the play of life, in the theatrics of living. Maybe Kramer knew deep down that we're all playing parts.

Jerry: This is as good as life gets. In this moment, there's no responsibility, which was extremely rare for me. When my friend Mario Joyner and I are together, everything we do has a single purpose: fun. Nothing is serious. We know it's not going to last, but for the time being it's a good living. Someone once asked what I enjoyed doing most in life. To me, it's just walking down the street joking around with a friend. It's so irresponsible and free.

Jerry: This might seem like a strange admission, coming after nine years on television, and it's pretty late in the game to be revealing it, but this is not what I do. I am not an actor. I am not a TV writer. I am not a producer. I am not an editor. I am not in casting. And I am not a leader of men. I am a comic. That is what I am comfortable doing.

I never figured on anything like my own television series. I didn't need it. I was overjoyed to be writing funny things and performing them for audiences. I was more than happy being a comic. What could be better than giving people a moment of laughter? Think about it. Laughter is a flash of perfection that lasts only a second or two. But like a surfer in the curl of a wave, when you're in a good one there's nothing better.

Julia: Sometimes it was difficult because I was the only girl and sometimes it was terrific because I was the only girl. Bottom line—I loved those guys. When you're shooting on the street, there's no studio audience, so you're trying to crack up the crew and the guys around the monitor. If I could make Jerry, Andy, and the writers laugh, that was like hitting it out of the park.

Jerry: Julia was the glamorous wacko. I like to think she liked me the best, but I'm not sure of it.

Jason: George's anger and insanity was sort of the whirlwind behind all the madness. Kramer's lunacy was a much saner lunacy. He just saw the world differently. George had no vision of the world and it drove him mad. The words and the attitude Larry, Jerry, and the writers gave me were delicious. I couldn't wait to make other people laugh by playing him.

Jerry: "The Puerto Rican Day" episode was a five-day "block and shoot" done entirely on location, which was something we hadn't done before. So in a way it wasn't a part of the series. The show before it was really the last episode, and this began the trip into another realm.

Jerry: This illustrates why Jerry and Elaine never got back together.

Jerry: I had 10,000 favorite things that I liked doing on the show itself, and certainly among them was telling George that he had a problem, especially one he wasn't aware of.

Michael: I always loved making Jerry laugh when we were working. It helped me settle in and to know I was part of the family.

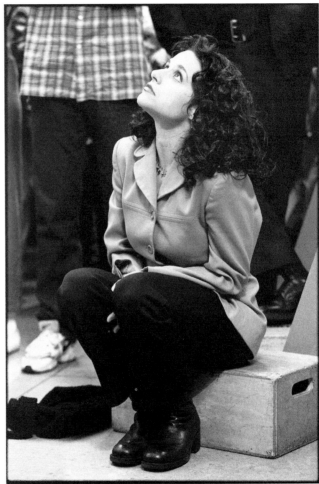

Julia: I've heard lots of women say, "I'm Elaine." I think they said it with a mix of frustration and humor. Geez, I hope they did. Elaine was someone who single women laughed at because she wrestled with their worst secrets and biggest fears. Let's face it, she embodied lots of problems. In fact, she was a jerk. I don't think she was a role model. I hope not. Anyone who chooses Elaine as a role model should be in therapy. People asked, "Are you like Elaine?" God no. She had gestures that weren't even mine and I don't know where they came from.

Michael: I worked out a routine where I have to light a sparkler and then use it to light my cigar. Then, while I'm talking, I toss the sparkler over my shoulder and it lands in the backseat of the car, inadvertently setting the Puerto Rican flag on fire. A lighter, a sparkler, lighting the cigar, tossing it, all while delivering about five lines as if I'm unaware of all the business. "It was an accident!" he shouted. Right.

Jerry: Every actor sits on a chair reading a script, but Michael does it differently. He works with the intensity of a bomb squad.

Michael: For years, people constantly said, "God, that '50s retro thing you're doing with the clothes is cool." But I made a point of saying his clothing was out of the '60s. His pants were short and the shirts were too tight because it was clothing he'd always owned. It was secondhand stuff. It was stuff Jerry'd given him. He'd take a sweater. He'd take a jacket. Or he'd buy stuff from thrift shops. Ten T-shirts for five bucks. Then he'd tell everyone how cheap they were, how cool they were. Maybe Kramer would give one away so someone else could be a part of the sale he'd found.

Julia: The media attention was otherworldly the last month or so. It reached a point where I would open a newspaper or magazine and expect to see my name. My picture showed up so often it became kind of normal, and that was very weird. Yet, amid all the attention, Katie Couric's visit to the set was oddly refreshing. We're from the same area back East and we always hit it off. She has a charisma and a charm that makes me feel as if I've known her my entire life. But most of America probably feels that way, too.

Jerry: Director Andy Ackerman, demonstrating perfect posture in this photo, was integral to the show. He was warm, lovable, funny, unflappable, and smart. He was like the intuitive mechanic who knew just how to make that four cylinder motor hum.

Jerry: Surrounded by writers Dave Mandel, Alec Berg, Jeff Schaffer, Jennifer Crittenden, director Andy Ackerman, and script supervisor Christine Nyhart, I said, "Something's not working here." As a result, my problem has become everyone's problem. Because we tried so hard to make each show as good as possible, we usually went from one problem to the next. Those little in-between moments when there was nothing to fix were precious and few.

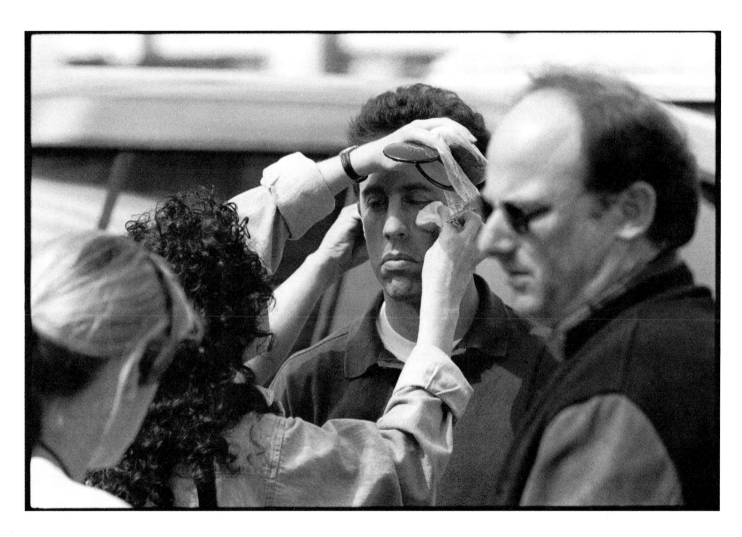

Jerry: As a performer, I learned that my appearance was something I had to get over. They would say, "Jerry, you don't look good today. We're going to put this little light in front of you to take the rings out from under your eyes." I'd say, "Fine, I don't care." So I don't look good. So what? I just wanted to know, "Did we get the shot? Can we move on?"

`Julia:` It often felt like we were sitting down to Thanksgiving dinner—like we'd known one another all our lives.

SEINFELD

"The Finale"

Written by

Larry David

Directed by

Andy Ackerman

Jerry: I felt the first hit of emotion when I drove to the studio early that Monday morning. But the dam really broke for me at the table read—the last time the cast and crew would sit at the long table and read through a brand-new script. Our places never changed—Julia was beside me and Jason was next to Michael.

Jerry: I wouldn't put "The Finale" into the category of fun. After nine years, how do you say good-bye to the experience, the people, the accomplishments? It was one of those major life transitions, like birth or death, where there's so much going on it becomes a little overwhelming. Human beings aren't designed to handle things so big. Emotionally, I just hoped not to get crushed, yet all the while I knew I would.

Julia: For the first time since the first episode, our parts were announced during the table read: "Michael Richards in the role of Kramer. Jason Alexander as George. Julia Louis-Dreyfus will be playing Elaine. And Jerry Seinfeld as Jerry." It was very poignant. As soon as I heard this, I was a goner.

Jerry: A person trying not to cry should not make another person laugh. Julia's crying, and I'm laughing at her and that's just wrong.

Larry David: I worked on the script for about a month. I started out thinking that I was going to miss the characters and I wanted to know where they would be. I wanted to have an image of them. I also wanted to leave open the possibility that they could come back, that they could emerge from somewhere. Not that they would come back and do the series, but just to perhaps give people some hope. You never know.

47

Jerry: Usually before I step in front of an audience, I slip into what comedians call "the bubble," that inner place where you close off from the rest of the world and get ready for the trip. Stand-up comedy is something that's created for the audience at the time they're seeing it. I hadn't done stand-up for a long time, so this wasn't easy. The only way stand-up gets easier is to perform it so often, you don't even realize what you're doing.

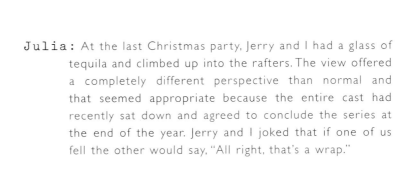

Julia: At the last Christmas party, Jerry and I had a glass of tequila and climbed up into the rafters. The view offered a completely different perspective than normal and that seemed appropriate because the entire cast had recently sat down and agreed to conclude the series at the end of the year. Jerry and I joked that if one of us fell the other would say, "All right, that's a wrap."

Jerry: I may not have slept there, but this apartment was where I lived. It was more real to me than my actual home. I spent more time there, which is a kind of weird way to live.

Julia: This is the angle from where we saw the show. We didn't watch it on TV or see it from the audience. We saw it right here.

Jerry: Hello, Newman.

Jerry: Wayne Knight was like a trip to the carnival. Something interesting was going on whenever you looked at him. Behind Wayne are scuff marks on the door that are the result of Kramer's entrances. Nine years' worth. We never had the door cleaned or painted.

Michael: I always felt that Kramer was poetic and soulful. The way I came through a door was somehow symbolic of how Kramer came to life. He swung into it. He came into it, fingers snapping, alive, swinging. It's what we all must do—take hold of ourselves, get into life, get involved, live. That sensibility became part of the attitude that governed this character. He was involved. An amazing kind of enjoyment dripped off him, and that's why I think people liked Kramer.

I'm known for entrances, which actually started me with an interest in making exits, but we always cut them because we never had time. Once I took up a piece of paper, and I said, "Well, I'm outta here." I grabbed the piece of paper off the table, it flew up in the air, and as I caught it, I fell out the back door where my foot caught the doorknob and closed the door behind me as the paper floated out. The audience was howling and there was this enormous applause. That would have been the best exit ever. An exit is another thing to explore, and I'll take these ideas with me to another character. But Kramer made a great entrance, didn't he?

Michael: The refrigerator, located just behind the set, was my altar. During the first season, I wrote "Funny" on it. For the last episode, someone added, "Le Fin." Between scenes, I kept my script atop it, and I always added some personal item of Kramer's. For the last day of shooting, I added his trophy. Somehow, it was the exclamation point of everything he'd been through.

Kramer went through a big evolution as far as I played him. When the show first came on the air, he was a few steps behind everybody else. I wouldn't know what the other characters were doing. In preparing each week, I would deliberately stay away from knowing the story lines. That way I would be surprised at seeing everything for the first time. I would always be trying to catch up. But in the middle of the thirteenth episode of the second year, I began to shift. I thought it would be more interesting to play the character as if he were a few steps ahead of everybody. So when I entered I already felt like I was on top of it, and then it was just a matter of finding out where everybody else was.

If everything about Kramer wasn't rehearsed, it was at least very well thought out. So when I finally went before the camera, I could let go and then all kinds of wonderful things could happen. It may have looked spontaneous, but I would always say, "Ah, a gift from the gods."

Michael: I always had thoughts other than what the scene directed me to do. I might have been thinking about a dirty ring around my tub and have that on my mind instead of what I'm saying in the scene. If we were in the coffee shop, I might be thinking about my car double parked outside while continuing to talk about all the femininas I saw at the beach. I believe that's the way we are in real life. You can be thinking one thing and saying another.

Jerry: If we had been a troupe of acrobats, Jason and I would have been the two guys at the bottom of the pyramid who hold everybody else up. Nine years after the pilot, we were still setting the whole thing in motion. Our attitude is the same. When I ask George what's the point of something if there's no joy, he tells me, "There is no point," and I think that is so funny. At the core, there's a very intimate connection here.

Jason: Over the years, the scenes got shorter and shorter because there were so many more of them. But *Seinfeld's* signature was the tangential runs of dialogue between George and Jerry that had nothing to do with the story, and early on that was unheard of in sitcom writing. Besides making people laugh, *Seinfeld* innovated a new structure to a genre that critics said was old and tired.

Jerry: The area between the couch and the counter was the key spot on the show. We had different names for it, like the Canyon of Heroes, the Wheelhouse, and Power Alley. All the action happened there. We just used the rest of the apartment to break things up.

Jerry: I think businesslike best describes the way I worked on the show. I had so much to do every second; it was that or die. I hate doing more than one thing at a time, and that's exactly what I did all day long every day for nine years. After a while, I'd say to myself, "Gee, I wonder what life was like in the '90s." I think I missed it.

Jerry: I always felt the responsibility to lead everyone—or at least try. I mean, I know it was my show and everything, but I never really wanted to be a boss of anything. Creating a show is a very symbiotic relationship. You create this thing, and then it starts creating you. Then it becomes like wrestling. You kind of roll around on the floor together. Sometimes it's on top, sometimes you're on top.

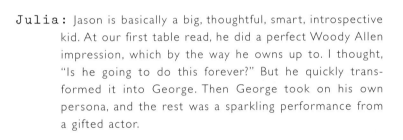

Julia: Jason is basically a big, thoughtful, smart, introspective kid. At our first table read, he did a perfect Woody Allen impression, which by the way he owns up to. I thought, "Is he going to do this forever?" But he quickly transformed it into George. Then George took on his own persona, and the rest was a sparkling performance from a gifted actor.

Jason: Jerry, Michael, and I strove to start Julia giggling—we lived for it. She is the most infectious giggler, especially when she's tired and it's late. I was always looking to do something to keep her feeling cute. No matter how late it was, Jerry would want to move on, but we were always having fun.

Jerry: My favorite work in the shows were always the two-man scenes. It was a throwback to being in a comedy team. Jason and I would joke, "We'll make them forget about Abbott and Costello."

Jerry: The show grew out of a friendship between me and *Seinfeld* co-creator Larry David (center). Our conversations were always funny explorations of the smallest, most arcane subjects, matters of such small importance they came to govern all of life. But that sensibility also defined how we made the show. The four of us did things in rehearsal that were so tiny you couldn't even see them on camera. I always felt like the show should be shot from a helmet camera because what I saw was even more amazing than what was on screen.

Julia: Scenes in the coffee shop were always great because we could sit and talk and enjoy one another's company. When we finally got around to doing the actual scene, there wasn't much work because all we had to do was sit there. We invented a lot of wonderful business because we were so loose and relaxed.

Jason: Jerry built a show that was thoroughly comfortable. Where are we? We're either sitting around an apartment or sitting in a coffee shop. That was the task. Whether the cameras were rolling or not, we sat around bullshitting. We had a strange camaraderie. During the nine years, we probably spent more time with one another than with our own families. At the end of each day we were ready to go home, but the next morning we were overjoyed to be with one another again. I think at times we might've taken it for granted that there would always be *Seinfeld*.

Jason: Michael never stopped looking for possibilities for his character. Here, I guarantee you, he was suggesting to Larry some sort of alternative approach. Meanwhile, Jeff Schaffer, one of the writers who ran the show after Larry left (seated next to Michael), was going through the script and probably saying to himself, "O.K. So this is a Larry David script." Larry was typically tense, but seemingly relaxed. Me? I have interrupted the discussion to say, "Don't worry, Larry. It's going to be great. It's funny. It's fun."

Michael: The real Kenny Kramer visited on the last day of shooting. Although Kenny told people that I based my character on him, that's not true. In the beginning, I plagued Larry David with questions about Kramer. How does this guy make a living? How much does he pay for his apartment? How long has he lived there? Who are his parents? Has he ever been married? Aside from telling me Kenny had lived across the hall from him and didn't have a job, Larry had no real answers. So I made it all up in my mind.

Michael: Norman Brenner was my stand-in for nine years. He's my guardian angel.

Julia: Our quick-change rooms were located directly behind the set. We'd go there to change between scenes. Jerry's is the first door. Mine is the last one. This was a very familiar 35-step walk that we often took together following a scene. It was our time to discuss how things went, what to expect next, or just to say, "Nice job." It was an intimate place, like the hallway in a college dorm.

Jerry: I was as interested in Michael off camera as on. He was a great storyteller, a wonderful comic, an all-around charmer. Whether it was a look, a roll of his eyes, or the way he stood, Michael was always doing something funny. What I'm going to miss most are those times when we cracked each other up in rehearsal.

Larry David: As Jerry would say, this is a big "George to Jerry" moment. Jerry is asking himself, "Why would I bring my idiot friend to this important meeting?" Certainly, that was true when we originally pitched the show to NBC. More important, we enjoyed each other's sense of humor, which is a prerequisite if you're going to write comedy with someone.

Jason: In the beginning, I admit, I thought Jerry was a relatively bad actor and a wonderful audience. He was always standing around on the set laughing at everyone else. I remember thinking, "Gosh, if this guy was watching out in TV-land we'd be a hit." Of course, Jerry became a better actor and remained the best audience.

Jason: I'd always lob the ball to Jerry Stiller and Estelle Harris, because I knew they would smash it back. In this scene for instance, I was thrilled that NBC liked the show that I was going to cowrite with Jerry. We were moving to California! Estelle shattered that dream with, "Since when do you know how to write? I never saw you write anything." Look at my body language. It says, "I'm wide open. Go ahead—strike and kill." I'd constantly throw myself in front of them like swine before wolves because I knew they'd always go for the jugular. They're two of the sweetest people in real life, but they were killers in terms of comedy.

Jerry: You can see here how cheap and makeshift it all was.

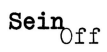

Jerry: Sure, we could've got someone taller, but again, as usual, I adjust.

Jerry: A meeting of the two comedy dons. We agreed the families must unite.

Larry David: It doesn't look like I was having much fun, does it? I enjoyed myself,
but I was very focused. I wanted to make
sure everything was right. The only thing
I still can't figure out is why I needed
such a heavy jacket.

89

Jerry: It was me and Larry, and then it was me and Jason. I don't know how I connected with each one of these people, but that's what was going on. So many relationships were made that worked. And that is what became the show. You had me and Jason, me and Michael, Michael and Julia, Michael and Jason, Julia and Jason—all those relationships worked. They were interesting to watch. It was like rolling seven fifteen times in a row.

Jason: As we did the show over the years, there was very little recognition among us that it was extraordinary. Jerry once said we were the world's biggest garage band. We were in the garage making noise and the neighborhood was saying, "These guys aren't bad." We were amusing ourselves. We knew we were celebrities. We knew we were making outrageous amounts of money. We knew we were doing something historical in the realm of TV. But it never infected anyone's attitude. It was our job, our playtime.

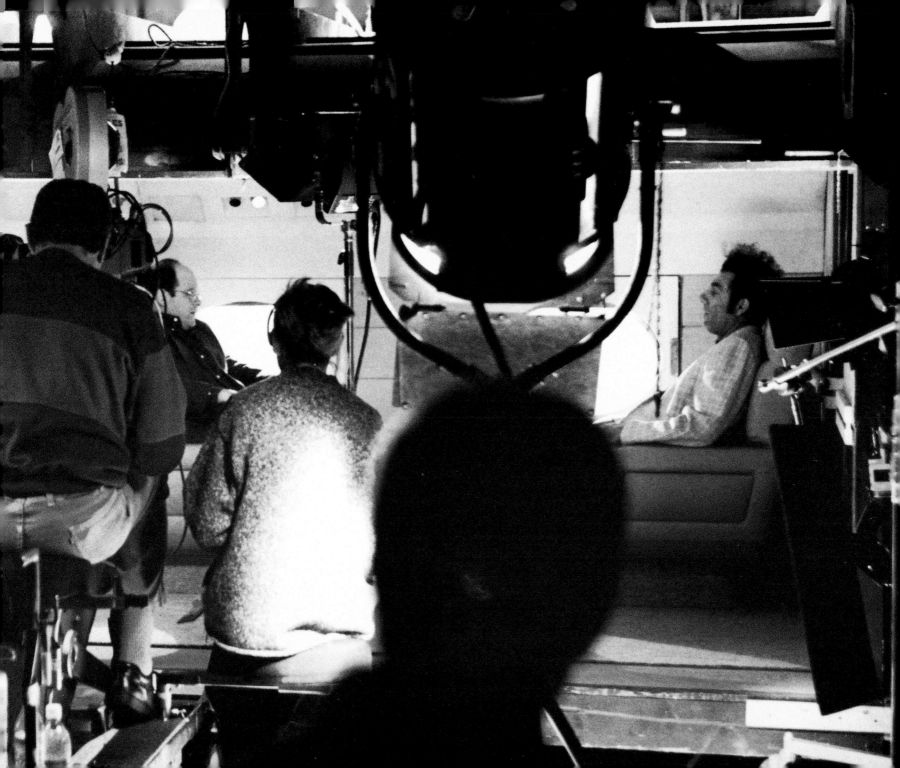

SEINFELD

B
CAM
V
2

A. ACKERMAN
W. KENNAN

4·13·98
04-7

Jerry: Like a scene from *The Twilight Zone*, Michael cut through the fatigue and tension of a long shoot by pretending we were really in the air and exclaiming in mock terror, "How did these people get on the wing?"

98

KRAMER STARTS HOPPING IN THE AISLE

           GEORGE
Kramer, what are you doing?

           JERRY
You've still got water in your ear?

           KRAMER
I can't get rid of it. Maybe it leaked
inside my brain.

           GEORGE
Kramer, would you stop that? It's not
safe to be jumping up and down on a
plane.

           KRAMER
I've got to get it out. I can't take
this anymore!

99

Jason: The stillness of this moment captures George's disappointment. We made it so funny, and it took so much time to get. Ironically, the shot didn't even make it into the episode. There was so much great footage left on the ground after nine years that no one will ever see.

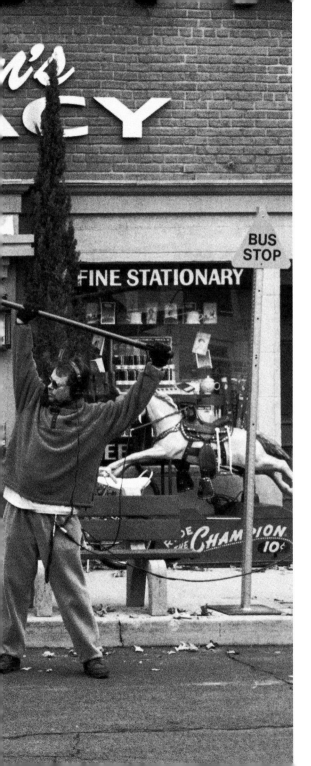

Larry David: I asked myself, "Where could I send them for a year or two with the possibility of them coming back?" The first thought was a biosphere. But that struck me as a little too crazy. Then I said, "Hey, what about prison?" They could be in jail for a year, then get out and everything would be the same. That led to another question: What can I send them to prison for?

Larry David: If the series was still on and someone had pitched this idea—that they were going to stand by while some guy got mugged and then make fun of him—I would've said, "No, it's too mean." And, in truth, it was the worst thing these characters have ever done. But because I wanted to get them arrested, it seemed like the best way.

Jerry: In almost any other setting, the four of us were very happy when stuck together. But this setup was a tough one.

Michael: I told Jerry on the very last episode, "This show isn't any easier than the first show," because I'd found Kramer in an entirely different situation. I asked myself, "How does Kramer function in a courtroom? How does he behave in jail? How does his view of life change from behind bars, if at all?" When Kramer had girlfriends, I had to ask, "How does he relate to a woman? What is his whole deal with a woman? How does he get on with a woman?" All that kind of thing was going on while I was working. Constantly.

Jerry: The perfect parents. Jerry Stiller was with Ed Sullivan and Barney Martin was with Jackie Gleason. That's good comedy DNA.

Julia: Our attorney Jackie Chiles, played wonderfully by Phil Morris, had that over-the-top opening statement to the court that cracked Jerry and me up every time. "Do you know what these four people were? They were innocent bystanders. Now you just think about that term, 'innocent bystanders.' Because that's exactly what they were. How can a bystander be guilty? Have you ever heard of a guilty bystander?" I put my hands over my face and pretended to cry, but I'm howling with laughter.

Michael: From the first show to the last, I wore Kramer's shoes during rehearsal. I wanted to feel his steps. In building the character, I wanted Kramer to be real and that never changed. Even though I pushed on him and made little sounds or faces, I always came back to a place where he was real. Nothing about Kramer was done solely for effect. It was all very personal.

Julia: The legal pads in front of us were filled with doodles. As each hour passed, the doodles became more obscene, immature, and hilariously funny. It was like being in school. We laughed when we weren't supposed to. There weren't any bigger fans of the show than the four of us. Like a lot of people at home, we loved seeing all these great characters from past shows enter the courtroom for one last shot at us.

Julia: It didn't take a lot for me to lose it. As the hours went on, I had real trouble controlling it. I laughed hysterically at the slightest provocation. If Jerry so much as smiled, I was gone. See how I'm leaning against him? We would all do that when we laughed hard. We'd lean or fall or bump into one another. It was a physical thing the four of us shared.

Jason: The show dealt with such detailed minutiae of life that everyone recognized themselves in the program. Most people don't work in a newsroom and fewer still work in an emergency room. Yet these situations are presented time and time again on television, and they're alien to most audiences. We were people who worked in an office or as an assistant to an assistant. Or we were between jobs. We lived in the city, went to the bank, parked our cars. People said, "I know what that's like." The show was about them. But we also said to the audience, "Don't worry about anything other than laughing. You don't have to invest in us as characters. You don't have to feel sorry for us. We don't grow. We don't learn. We are only here to make you laugh."

Michael: Kramer didn't crack up. Once I climbed into his presence, it was hard for me to break. I was in character. I was channeling Kramer. The others would always crack up at a little piece of business, some accident that could never be re-created. Kramer would look at them like they're crazy. Why are you laughing?

I did a bit one time with a pipe. It was one of those moments beyond the work, when you let it go before the camera and wonderful things happen. A piece of thread was stuck to a pipe as I pulled it out of my pocket, and when I pulled the thread it popped the tobacco out of the pipe. Then when I moved my hand to catch the tobacco, it swung the pipe around. It did all this nice movement, and I had to catch the pipe—still with the thread. Julia was standing there and she cracked up, then everyone laughed and the director said, "All right, CUT!" I turned and said, "I wish to God you guys hadn't gone up, because there is no way I will ever be able to re-create that piece of business."

Julia: In the midst of trying to concentrate during yet another late night, I called home and organized what my children were having for dinner. How surreal was that? While the world fixated on this last episode, I just wanted to get some macaroni and cheese on the table.

James Rebhorn
(D.A. Hoyt)
and
Wendel Meldrum
(The Low Talker)

It was Seinfeld co-creator Larry David who provided the faceless voice of George Steinbrenner in the episodes when George Costanza worked for the Yankees.

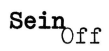

John Pinette
(Howie)

Teri Hatcher
(Sidra Holland)

Grace Zabriskie
(Mrs. Ross)

Reni Santoni
(Poppy)

Julia: Between scenes, it felt like a wedding. People from our past kept showing up. We hadn't seen some of these actors for years. Then someone like the Rye Lady or the Bubble Boy would appear and I'd think, "My God, that show was before I had my first son." It heightened the nostalgia as we said good-bye to one kind of life and moved into another.

Donna Evans
(Woman from the Handicap Spot)

John Hayman
(Donald Sanger, The Bubble Boy)

Richard Fancy
(Mr. Lippman)

Robert Katims
(Mr. Deansfry)

David Byrd
(Pharmacist)

Ian Abercrombie
(Mr. Pitt)

Carlos Jacott
(Pool Guy)

Miguel Sandoval
(Marcelino)

David Dunard
(Security Guard)

Philip Baker Hall
(Bookman, The Library Cop)

Victor Raider-Wexler
(Dr. Wexler)

Tony Carlin
(Elaine's Co-worker)

INT.COURTROOM-LATER.

D.A. AT HIS DESK.

                    D.A. HOYT
Call Yev Kassem to the stand.

                    BAILIFF
Call Yev Kassem.

                    JERRY
Who?

ANGLE ON: DOORS OPEN. YEV ENTERS.

                    ELAINE
The Soup Nazi!

                    JACKIE CHILES
Soup Nazi? You people have a little
pet name for everybody.

                                DISSOLVE TO:

INT. COURTROOM - MOMENTS LATER
SOUP NAZI ON THE STAND.

                    D.A. HOYT
State your name.

                    YEV
Yev Kassem.

                    D.A. HOYT
Could you spell that please?

                    YEV
No. Next question.

Sheree North
(Babs Kramer)

Jane Leeves
(Marla Penny, The Virgin)

Frances Bay
(Mabel Choate, The Marble Rye Lady)

Brian George
(Babu Bhatt)

Julia: I thought Michael was nuts when I first met him. I didn't know how to deal with him. He's very much in his own world, which is both his style and his strength. But now that I've been to his world, I can honestly say it's a good world. During the show's first season, I would've been too intimidated to tease him like this. But now I can give him as much grief as I want and he takes it without a problem. I loved to make him laugh.

Jerry: I think our ability to draw together disparate types was a key element to the show's success.

INT. JACKIE CHILES' HOTEL ROOM - DAY

TWO FIGURES IN BED. WE SEE JACKIE. HE
ROLLS OVER. WE SEE HE'S WITH SIDRA.

                    SIDRA
Oh Jackie. You're so articulate.

                JACKIE CHILES
We got plenty of time too. This jury
could be out for days.

SFX: PHONE RINGS. JACKIE ANSWERS.

            JACKIE CHILES (CONT'D)
Hello? ...Damn. (HE HANGS UP)
They're ready.

HE WINCES.

MONDAY, APRIL 6, 1998

CAST

NEWMAN, HERNANDEZ, RABBI, MORTY, HELEN, FRANK, ESTELLE, UNCLE LEO, MICKEY, BANIA, PUDDY, PETERMAN, WILHELM, MR+MRS. ROSS, BABS KRAMER GUARD, JERRY, JASON, JULIA, MICHAEL, JACKIE, DA HOYT, ASS. DA, BAILIFF, JUDGE V (JURY, STENOGRAPHER, FOREMAN, SUSIE, ATMOS) VOGEL, HOWIE (JAY, STU), MABEL, MR. PITT, SANGER, DONALD MARLA, DR. WEXLER, DET. HERSON, SIDRA, ROBIN, DEENSFREI, DET. BLAKE, BOOKMAN, SEC. GUARD WOMAN, LIPPMAN, PHARMACIST, CO-WORKER, POOL GUY, POPPY, LOW TALKER, YEV, BABU, MARCELINO, STEINBRENNER.

Jerry: Do we look guilty?

Jerry: Very guilty.

Julia: Working with Andy Ackerman (left), nothing is tense or impossible. He is a very liberating director.

Jason: Larry David (above) has tremendous faith in his ability and talent, as well he should, but it is mixed with equal amounts of incredible self-doubt and self-hate.

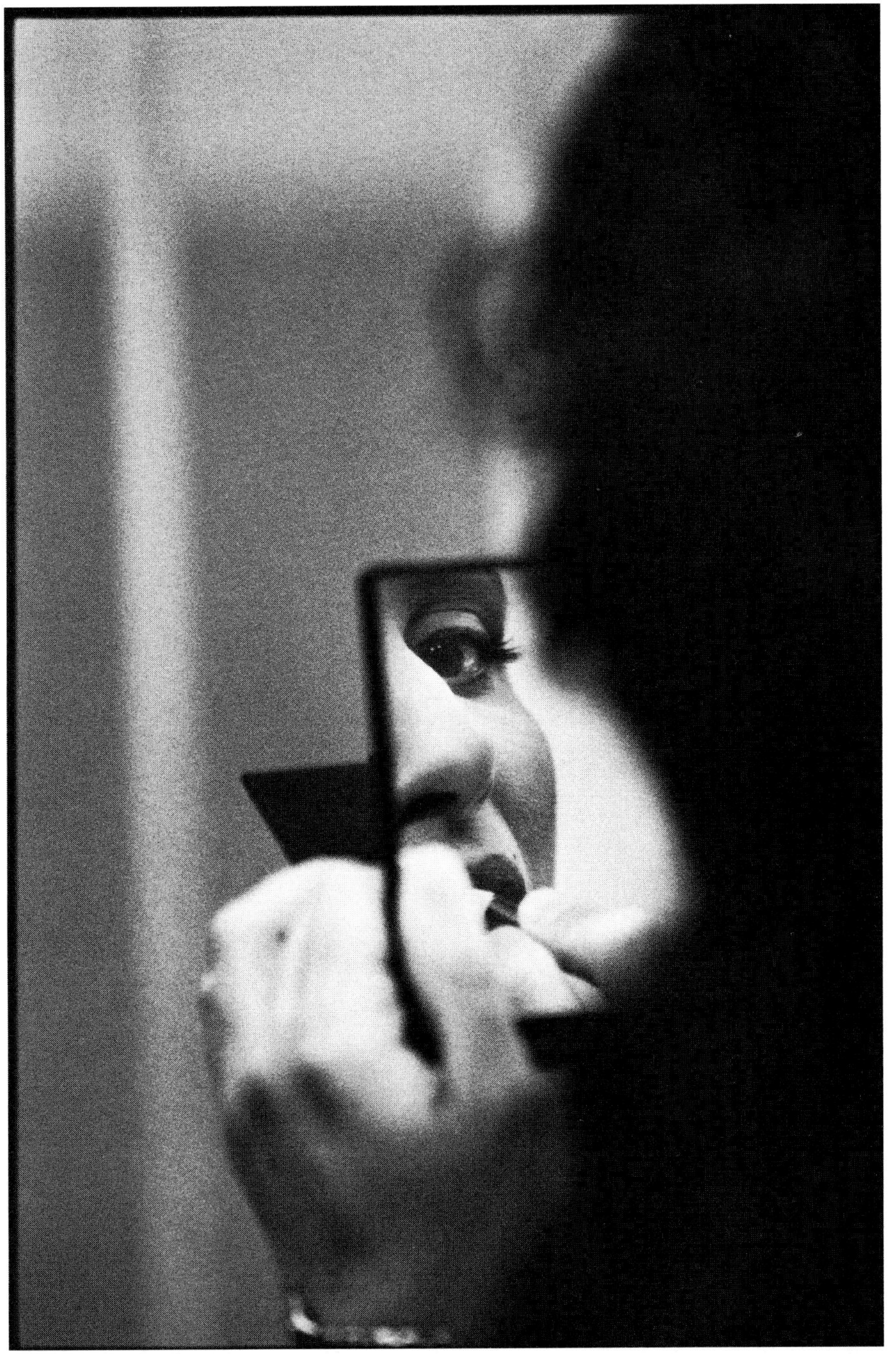

Jerry: I missed the audience. If I could've seen the audience, I might not have wanted to stop. But I couldn't grasp an audience of 35 million people. I don't know what that would look like. I couldn't hear the laughter the way I can when I'm onstage in a club. Feeling an audience's joy excites me more than ratings. It's what I'm willing to work for.

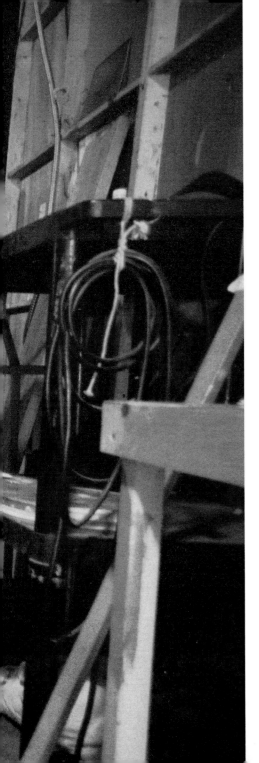

Julia: Before each show, the four of us always huddled back-
stage. Normally we held hands and shouted, "Circle of
power!" then growled like football players. It sent us onstage laughing. But this last huddle was an emotional
killer. Instead of the normal routine, Jerry said, "Because
of what we've done together, we'll always be inexorably
linked in people's minds. And I couldn't be happier about
with whom I'm going to be inexorably linked." Well, as
soon as he began to speak, he started to weep. Then I
lost it. Actually, we were all overcome with emotion. It
was strangely comforting because he made me realize we
would never have to say good-bye to one another. It was
a lovely moment, and it felt very right.

Jason: Although we had voted to end our collaboration, we
could never end our relationship. Despite how different
we are as individuals, we melded into this thing that
worked more beautifully and joyfully than anything I will
probably ever be part of again. It helped to think that the
experience of what we had created would last beyond
our lives. But at the time, we knew the four of us would
never combine forces again to make this magic, and that
was what we were going to miss.

Michael: I always thought Kramer should get on a kick to leave the city. Leave the other three and go on some quest for adventure where he would discover himself in relation to nature. In this next incarnation, I saw him as a kind of *Kung Fu* type of character, going into small towns the way he came through the door at Jerry's and getting into all sorts of trouble. I saw him hanging out with truckers. Maybe falling in love with a Native American woman and getting run off the reservation for burning down a cornfield. I also would've loved to see Kramer go foreign. He was fascinated with geisha girls. He could've gone to Japan and talked with them. "They're great talkers, Jerry. They know everything about anything."

Then he would've come back in some crazy way better informed—but not really. He'd just be able to keep on talking about life. I always loved the end of *Crocodile Dundee* where the hero departs on a "walkabout." I pictured Kramer crossing over the bridge into New Jersey, turning briefly to wave good-bye, like Chaplin.

Jerry: It was important to the four of us that we be together for the final shot. Jail was a fine place for that.

INT. LATHAM COUNTY PRISON - DAY

JERRY ONSTAGE, DOING STAND-UP. THE PRISON POPULA-
TION MAKES UP THE AUDIENCE.

JERRY
So what is the deal with the yard? I mean when I
was a kid, my mother wanted me to play in the
yard, but of course she didn't have to worry
about your next door neighbor, Tommy, sticking a
shiv in my thigh.

SILENCE, EXCEPT FOR KRAMER, WHO IS LAUGHING.

JERRY (CONT'D)
And what's with the lock-down? Why do we have to
be locked in our cells? Are we that bad that we
have to be sent to prison in prison? You would
think the weight lifting and sodomy is enough.

KRAMER BURSTS OUT IN LAUGHTER AGAIN.

AS THE GUARD ESCORTS JERRY OFF, THE CROWD BOOS.

JERRY (CONT'D)
See you in the cafeteria!

FADE OUT.

END OF SHOW

Michael: The show really did end at the right time. Had it ended a year or two earlier, I would have thought we'd lost out. Had it continued, I probably would've thought we pushed it too far. But at the end of this nine, we knew that we'd done it. There was no sadness for me, only joy.

Jason: We had all been through a lot the past couple of seasons. First, Larry left, which presented new difficulties. Then we went through the contract renegotiations, which caused lots of tension and despair. The foundation of the show was threatened each time but we got through it all. Then we went through this season knowing it was the end. There was a ton of emotion, yet we weren't an emotional group, and consequently, nothing got expressed. All we did was make jokes. But after that last line, we allowed ourselves to admit what we had done was truly extraordinary. We suddenly turned into a blubbering group of people hugging and kissing, "Hey, I love you, man. I'm going to miss you."

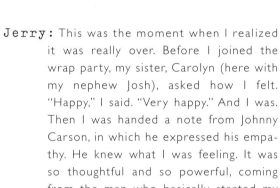

Jerry: This was the moment when I realized it was really over. Before I joined the wrap party, my sister, Carolyn (here with my nephew Josh), asked how I felt. "Happy," I said. "Very happy." And I was. Then I was handed a note from Johnny Carson, in which he expressed his empathy. He knew what I was feeling. It was so thoughtful and so powerful, coming from the man who basically started my career.

Julia: I was unprepared when Jerry handed the microphone to me at the wrap party. I expressed what I think all of us were feeling. I thanked Jerry for sharing the spotlight with us. Though Jerry was smiling (he'd lose it later), we were all crying buckets. For as unsentimental, cynical, and dark as our characters were drawn, personally we were the opposite.

Jason: After Jerry said a simple thank-you, Julia and I both got up and said, "No, thank *you*. Because you don't hear that enough."

Jerry: Julia and I always liked watching the gag reel together at the wrap parties. Every year we made sure to sit next to each other. The fun we got from watching twenty minutes of us goofing off and messing up captured the joy we had working together. It almost made the whole season worth it. This last year was full of mistakes. I think it was the best ever.

Scrapbook

If it wasn't for Maynard Parker, the editor of *Newsweek*, the photographs in this book would never have been taken. In 1996, Maynard took me onboard at the magazine as a contributing editor. Since then I've done special photographic assignments for him from *Seinfeld* to Sarajevo. Working with Maynard and the other wonderful folks at *Newsweek* is a joy. Thanks to you all.

And thanks to:

Jerry, Julia, Michael, Jason, and Larry, who for a few precious weeks took me into their special world to document the last golden moments of *Seinfeld*. Your family scrapbook is finally finished!

Maureen Erbe, Rita Sowins, and Efi Latief of Erbe Design in South Pasadena, California. Maureen's cover design and fantastic layouts are a compliment to both the photos and text.

Jain Lemos, an astonishingly talented picture editor whose dedication, organized thinking, and incredible work ethic are the reasons this book actually got finished.

Todd Gold, Mauro DiPreta, and Susan Weinberg Editors.

Dan Strone and Owen Laster of the William Morris Agency. They are the top of their field and were involved from start to finish.

Jeff MacNelly, who loves skewering his buddies on the end of his pen.

Castle Rock Entertainment, especially Glenn Padnick, Jess Wittenberg, and publicist-in-chief Elizabeth Clark.

Seinfeld producers Nancy Sprow, Tim Kaiser, and Susan Greenberg. Nancy's work on this book was above and beyond the call of duty.

Wayne Kennan, director of photography on the show. His lighting made my photos look like a million bucks. Randy Carter, 1st AD, UPM, good guy, and the rest of the *Seinfeld* crew. Dan Zaitz and Carin Baer, photographic colleagues who provided me with great technical advice on the set. Carol Brown, Jerry's assistant, who always knew where I could corral Jerry. Pros one and all.

166

My family. Heartfelt appreciation and love to my wife, Rebecca, who has gone through the wars with me. And to my three sons, Byron, Nicholas, and the latest arrival, Jack, who was born just after the last *Seinfeld* episode wrapped.

Special appreciation to:

Alain Labbe, Arnaud Gregori, Virginia Smith, Rodney White, Daniel Bald, and the rest of the crew at Paris Photo in Los Angeles. All of my Kodak Tri-X film was processed there, and the magnificent prints were made by David Healey.

Dave Metz of Canon USA. These photographs were taken using the *Canon EOS-1n* cameras. Since switching to Canons, photography has once again become a delight.

Dirck Halstead, my friend and fellow photog, who has launched the best Website in photojournalism at www.digitaljournalist.org, where you can catch some of my *Seinfeld* pictures.

John Glenn, who at 77 will be orbiting the earth about the same time that this project is launched. John and his wife Annie got an early peek at these pictures in Houston, and told me they can't wait to see the book!

And finally, thanks and affection to *Seinfeld* executive producers George Shapiro and Howard West. Howard dealt with the initial difficulties of producing this book. Without him, it would not have seen the light of day.

—David Hume Kennerly

1: Wayne Kennan (Director of Photography) 2: Michael, Jerry, and Michele Correy 3: Jennifer Crittenden (Co-producer) and Jerry 4: Tim Wawrzeniak (1st Assistant Camera) 5: Christine Nyhart (Script Supervisor) 6: Larry David, Nancy Sprow (Coordinating Producer) and Jerry 7: Tim Kaiser (Producer) and Skip Collector (Editor)

167

Scrapbook

8: Ed Nielsen (Camera Operator) and Bob Apger (2nd Assistant Camera) **9:** Jeff Miller, Deck McKenzie, Peggy Lane-O'Rourke, and Norman Brenner (Stand-ins) **10:** Michael, Lesley Robins, (Set Assistant) and Jerry **11:** Teri Hatcher and Tom "TK" Keith (2nd 2nd AD) **12:** Randy Carter (UPM/1st AD) **13:** Elza Camacho and Dennis Kirkpatrick (Boom Operators) **14:** Jeff Miller (Camera Operator) and David Tolsky (1st Assistant Camera)

15: Jerry and Peter Mehlman (former *Seinfeld* writer) **16:** Jason with wife, Daena **17:** Lauren Bowles (Monk's Waitress, Julia's sister) **18:** Alec Berg, Larry David, Jeff Schaffer, and Dave Mandel (Writers) **19:** Julia and J. T. Krul (Production Coordinator) **20:** Mike "Spike" Ryan (Dolly Grip)

Scrapbook

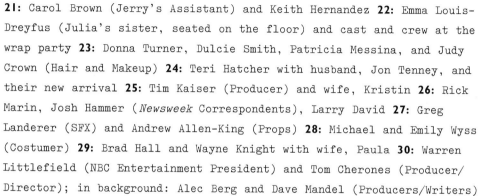

21: Carol Brown (Jerry's Assistant) and Keith Hernandez **22:** Emma Louis-Dreyfus (Julia's sister, seated on the floor) and cast and crew at the wrap party **23:** Donna Turner, Dulcie Smith, Patricia Messina, and Judy Crown (Hair and Makeup) **24:** Teri Hatcher with husband, Jon Tenney, and their new arrival **25:** Tim Kaiser (Producer) and wife, Kristin **26:** Rick Marin, Josh Hammer (*Newsweek* Correspondents), Larry David **27:** Greg Landerer (SFX) and Andrew Allen-King (Props) **28:** Michael and Emily Wyss (Costumer) **29:** Brad Hall and Wayne Knight with wife, Paula **30:** Warren Littlefield (NBC Entertainment President) and Tom Cherones (Producer/Director); in background: Alec Berg and Dave Mandel (Producers/Writers)

171

31: Jerry and Judy Kerr (Dialogue Coach) **32:** Back row: Gerard Brown, Kevin Jackson, Eric Felder, Wesley Thompson, Gregg Dickerson; Front row: Jaime Perry, Raoul Roach (Extras), and Jerry **33:** Charmaine Simmons (Costume Designer) and Larry David **34:** Nancy Sprow and Suzy Greenberg (Producers) **35:** Michael and Chris Heath (*Rolling Stone* Reporter) **36:** Pete Berkson (1st Assistant Camera) and Pete Papanickolas (Key Grip) **37:** Jerry and Elizabeth Clark (Castle Rock Publicist) **38:** George Shapiro and Howard West (Executive Producers/Jerry's Managers) **39:** The last *Seinfeld* script

Good
Bye